Anxiety, Leave Me Alone

Simple Ways To End Anxiety Now

By Alex Canny

COPYWRIGHT

Table of Contents

Introduction

It is possible to manage your anxiety and live life to the fullest. Having anxiety is not a medical condition. Anxiety is just a feeling that is generated from our distorted perception of reality. If we can change our perception, we can change our feeling.

This book is devoted to transforming your perception of anxiety triggers. It will guide you toward resilience to feelings that bring distress. You'll learn the cognitive and behavioral strategies to face your fears head-on and conquer them with confidence. You'll also learn how to make peace with distressing thoughts and take their power away so that they can't bother you anymore.

Methods included in this book are very effective. However, each chapter of this book is meant to build on what was covered in the earlier chapters. Therefore make sure not to skip any chapter.

Chapter 1

Discovering the Origin of Your Anxiety

Our journey of overcoming anxiety will start with exploring the origins of the sense of irrational dread. The feeling of anxiety is harmless, although it can make you feel extremely uncomfortable. We all have different anxiety triggers. If you can identify your own anxiety trigger, you can apply the right tool to manage your anxiety.

Exploring your anxiety triggers can illuminate the origins of your anxiety. Understanding the origin will help you to embrace the symptoms to diminish their power. When you develop self-acceptance, you will stop criticizing yourself for having this emotion, and direct your energy from fighting the feeling, toward doing something productive with your life. Fighting the anxiety or running away from anxiety will only make your anxiety stronger.

In some cases, finding the origin of your anxiety can be useful to eliminate the root cause of your problem. For instance, if the origin of your anxiety is an abusive relationship, a demanding work environment or financial problems, you can take steps to fix those issues. However, not all sources can be diminished. If anxiety originates from the traumatic memories of the past or if it develops gradually from childhood, there is nothing you can do to eliminate the root cause. In those cases, you have to learn how to make peace with painful memories.

For many people, finding the actual cause for their anxiety can be difficult, even impossible. If you know the root cause of your anxiety and you also know a solution, then use the solution to break free from the confines of anxiety.

If you don't know the origin of your anxiety, there is nothing to worry. Methods we are going to learn in this book will work regardless of your level of knowledge of the origin.

The very first step to managing an emotion is to recognize it. But sometimes identifying an unwanted feeling and emotion can be difficult for some people. There are a few reasons behind it. One of the major reasons is the avoidance tendency.

As avoidance provides temporary relief, some people develop creative ways to avoid their anxiety. Here are some common avoidance behaviors:

- "Workaholism" in which people always remain engaged in working to avoid unpleasant emotions.
- "Denial and repression" where people either try to resist their emotion or pretend nothing has happened.

- " Sensation seeking " in which people involve sensation-producing activities such as compulsive gambling.
- " Alcoholism and substance abuse " in which, people seek temporary riddance in alcohol and drugs.

Although avoidance behavior is a temporary fix, a very high level of fear avoidance is a risk factor for long-term anxiety.

However, if you have an avoidance tendency like most people, you can use it to manage your anxiety symptoms. In this case, you have to find a " distraction " or an activity that is creative and entertaining, to cover up your bad feelings. But you have to make sure not to overdo it.

Remember, avoiding your anxiety or seeking ways to escape your anxiety is never a permanent solution. If you keep avoiding your own feeling, it may resurface more powerfully and make you feel miserable. That's why it is important to deal with them head-on.

Recognize your feelings and emotions and observe them to gain insight into the nature of your condition. When you can identify the emotion and the factors that cause that emotion, you can challenge it.

However, it is all right if you can't clearly identify your feeling. Some people are so connected with their mind and emotions that they can notice even the slightest change in the feeling. Others can develop this awareness with practice.

If you want to develop your awareness of your feeling and emotion, assess your current mood: How do you feel right now? Notice the pace of your breathing. Is your breathing slow and deep or fast and shallow? Notice the posture of your body. Is the position of your body relaxed and comfortable? Do you feel any tightness or heaviness or any other sensations in any part of your body? What feeling can you associate with those sensations? If you are not experiencing any strong sensations and your breath is normal and your body is relaxed, notice what it feels like to be relaxed. If you are having a strong sensation, label this sensation and notice what it feels like having this sensation.

Notice the emotions you're experiencing right now. Do you feel nervous, panicked, irritated, angry, sad, insecure, timid, upright, self-conscious, disturbed or uneasy? Think the word that captures the essence of the feeling in your mind. You don't need to do anything about them. The goal is to identify your feelings and feel more connected with your body and mind. The best method to develop awareness is mindfulness meditation, which we will learn in the upcoming chapters.

Developing Thought Awareness

Thoughts and emotions are closely linked — They have a cause-effect relationship. What you think is reflected in your feeling. What you feel is reflected in your thoughts. A feeling is a single emotion. To get a hold of your anxiety, you have to be aware of both of your thoughts and feelings. If you can uncover the thoughts that contribute your anxious feelings, you can re-program your thought patterns and transform your anxiety into calmness.

Feel your thoughts. Feeling the thoughts does not mean that thoughts can be felt the same way you feel hot and cold. Just as some people are unaware of what they are feeling, others have difficulties knowing what goes in their mind when they are nervous, tensed or anxious. What we feel and what we think are more intimately connected than most of us know.

Sometimes during the therapy sessions for anxiety, the therapists asks the patient what they are thinking when they feel nervous or tensed. Patients often describe their feelings rather than their thoughts. It's probably because often during the moments of anxiety, we don't have a clearly identifiable thought. Here the goal is to discover what the anxiety triggering situation means to you. That will show what your thoughts are.

Think about a situation that makes you upset. Now, in your mind's eye, see the whole picture, and find out which part of that event triggers upsetting emotions. Some of us feel anxious even before the anxiety-producing event takes place. Find out which aspects of that particular situation are perceived as stressful in your mind. Is it a thought or image of fear of the anticipated future event?

Sometimes people with acute anxiety disorder wake up in the middle of the night with intense dread. What could be the trigger in this? We can find the answer through self-inquiry.

A simple exercise can improve your thought awareness. When you get anxious or worried, take a moment to reflect. Find out what thoughts or images appear in your mind right before the anxious feeling. If you can identify them, then you've found the triggers of your anxious feelings.

Remember, an event itself can't make you anxious— it is how you perceive that particular event that brings forth the emotion. Your thoughts reflect the meaning the event holds for you.

Thoughts bring pleasure and pain. Observe the thoughts that crowd your mind when you feel upset, and notice how they activate your anxiety.

Take time to contemplate on the triggering thoughts and images that bring dreadful feelings. Ask yourself "what part of the event makes me feel anxious?" "What is the worst that could happen?" "If the worst happened what impact it would have had on my life?" "Could this affect people's view about me? How?" "Did I relate this event with something in the past that bothered me? Take time to get this answers.

Educate yourself about the nature of your own anxiety. If it doesn't help you to rise above the anxiety, it will definitely help you to live with it.

Observing Your Triggering Thoughts

We all have different patterns of anxiety. The moment you focus on your triggering thoughts, the process of paying attention will bring thought process to light. You will understand your own anxiety pattern and gain a new perspective to adopt the right strategy to manage your anxiety. Monitor your triggering thoughts and feelings any time in any situation.

Maintain a notebook to keep records of anxious trigger thoughts and feelings. Rate your anxiety level from 1 to 100, where 1 is the state of almost no-anxiety, and 100 is the state of highest anxiety possible.

Here is an example:

Anxiety triggers: Today my boss was mad at me because I made a careless error.

Anxious thoughts: My career is over. I'm such an idiot!

Feelings and sensations: Fear, guilt, frustration, anger.

Anxiety rating: 80

Once you are done writing, look at the thoughts and ask yourself, " does this situation really pose any actual threat or am I blowing thing out of proportion?" If you're not sure whether your trigger thoughts are rational look for the pieces of evidence to support your thought — find out if the thoughts hold water. If no evidence is found, then there is no need to trust these thoughts. Every time you question a trigger thought, you'll start taking them less seriously and your anxiety level will shrink.

Practice this exercise every day. You may not notice any immediate effect in the beginning. But after practicing for a few weeks, you'll discover that your trigger thoughts are no longer upsetting you.

The Voice of Anxiety

During the moments of anxiety, we experience negative chatter. While confronting an anxiety-producing situation, if we engage ourselves in negative self-talk patterns, we may feel trapped into a never-ending cycle of harmful thoughts, which can make our anxiety from bad to infinitely worse.

Do you become aware of your own negative inner-dialogues when you feel stressed or worried? These automatic negative thoughts keep bubbling up when people experience persistent anxiety. The experiencer feels as if he or she is trapped in a vicious cycle and there is no escape.

The Human brain produces anywhere between 25,000 and 50,000 thoughts an a day.

If the mind is trapped in negativity, imagine how many negative thoughts it experiences everyday — thousands upon thousands!

Negative thoughts activate the release of stress hormones into our system. These hormones speed up our thought, our heartbeats, and various other physiological functions, which make our situation even worse.

Pay attention to the inner-conversation that goes on in the mind when you feel anxious. These are the voices of anxiety. This is what your anxiety sounds like. These inner-dialogues create illusion and make us believe in it. In his book, David Burns, a clinical psychologist at the Stanford University School of Medicine said, " People who are anxious and depressed are often masters of illusion. Their pessimistic outlook and some unconscious tricks of the mind can turn triumphs into setbacks, and setbacks into personal feelings."

Negative thoughts emerge from the depth of our mind when we are overwhelmed with anxiety. They slip into the brain under the radar of conscious awareness and turns into powerful habitual patterns. They arise automatically before we do anything to stop them. We may not be able to prevent them from occurring, but we can change our perception about the anxiety triggers. When the perception changes, everything changes.

You have more control over your thoughts than you think you have. If you can detect the words of your anxiety and restructure your anxious thoughts you can liberate yourself from those negative thought patterns.

Understanding the Nature of Negative Thought Patterns

Negative thought patterns are not always easy to detect. But if you want to manage the negative emotions of anxiety, you need some understanding of your distorted thought patterns. Once you learn about the thought patterns of anxiety, you can reframe them to be positive in nature and create a better reality. There are ten major thinking patterns or cognitive biases that trigger your anxious feeling:

Black and White thinking

When you're engaged in this thinking pattern, you will believe that you should do a thing perfectly or don't do at all. You'll feel an inner demand to be a perfectionist. You will have high expectations of yourself, which may motivate you to work hard to achieve perfection, but at the same time, it will discourage you to try new things because you might not do it perfectly. Black and white thinking make us believe that we are never good enough — which makes us feel inadequate, and generate a feeling of anxiety. When you become aware of a 'black and white' thought, say to yourself, "I am thinking black and white. These thoughts are irrational. This is the voice of anxiety".

Overgeneralization

Overgeneralization is a logical fallacy, which occurs when you use a small even insignificant example to generalize everything. For instance, if you fail to perform well in a small competition, overgeneralization will try to make you believe that you'll fail in every competition that comes your way. This negative propensity of the mind makes us see any negative situation that occurs as being an unlimited pattern of setbacks and defeat. Overgeneralization is a very common thinking pattern that goes through the minds of anxious people. When you find yourself overgeneralizing, say to yourself, "I'm overgeneralizing. These thoughts are irrational. This is the voice of anxiety".

Selective abstraction

This negative bias occurs when we feel that the negative outweighs the positive in life. When you engage in selective abstraction, you only dwell on the negative aspect of a situation no matter how insignificant it is, and unwittingly overlook all the positive aspects. It's like you're wearing a pair of glasses designed to filter out all the bright sights and let you see only the negative aspects. This causes unnecessary sufferings.

Selective abstraction has the potential to turn a negative thought into a self-fulfilling prophecy. When you constantly focus and rehearse on the dark side of something, you're unwittingly acting to make it more real. As, for example, if a person with social anxiety constantly thinks that they will blush while approaching new people, then that very thought will trigger blushing. When you find yourself engaging in selective abstraction, say to yourself, "Wait a minute! I'm not seeing the whole picture. There must be something good about this situation. I'm not going to let the voice of anxiety put me down!"

Disqualifying the positive

Have you heard about the alchemists who dreamt about inventing a method to transmute any base metal into gold? Negative thoughts can make you do the exact opposite— that is turning your golden joy into an emotional lead. This is why psychologist David. D. Burns termed that thought pattern as, " reverse alchemy".

When you disqualify the positive, you twist something positive into a negative. Here is an example— you've passed the test, but you think you passed only because the test was easy. If you disqualify the positive, you can't explain a thing rationally, because you're using a double standard. People, who engage in this thinking pattern, only count the negative pieces of evidence no matter how irrational or irrelevant they sound and reject the positive evidence no matter how strong and persuasive they seem. If you find yourself indulging in this thought pattern, say to yourself, "I think I'm paying more attention to the negative aspects, where there are lots of positive things to focus on".

Jumping to conclusions

This thinking pattern and anxiety often go hand in hand. When we have anxiety, we tend to come to a conclusion based on inadequate evidence, and these conclusions are often wrong and usually negative. Sometimes we even quickly evaluate a person or situation based on some beliefs, which has no basis. We often don't feel the need to enquire the fact before believing the negative mental chatter. Jumping to conclusion thought patterns fall into two categories — one is mindreading another is fortune telling.

Mindreading is a very common issue among people with social anxiety. They often tend to make the false assumptions that some people are looking down on them or thinking they are stupid or boring. They simply can't resist the impulse of assuming what others are thinking about them. If you catch yourself having the thoughts like, my co-worker thinks I'm wired or she thinks I'm a loser, instead of absolutes, rephrase the statements as a possibility (like he/ she might think). You can also replace mindreading thoughts with a less rigid statement, like, "I can be an intelligent person, and still do something stupid". Or you can dismiss those theories altogether using strong phrases like, " So what!" or "Who cares!"

Fortunetelling is common among all anxiety types. When people have persistent anxiety, they look ahead to the future and see only misery. They think no matter how much they try they will end up in failure. They mentally repeat false predictions about their future and turn them into powerful beliefs, which worsens their anxiety. If you find yourself engaging in jumping to conclusion thought pattern, say to yourself, "I recognize the thought pattern — this is jumping to conclusion. I'm not going to believe what anxiety tries to make me believe. Instead, I choose to have a rational talk with myself".

Magnification and Minimization

Another name of this thought pattern is "binocular trick". If you look through an inverted binocular, you'll see everything far away and smaller. That's what anxiety does. Our anxious mind tricks us to see negative things far bigger than they actually are and positive things insignificantly small — it is as if we are wearing special lenses. When you give in to binocular trick you subconsciously put proportionately greater emphasis on a perceived failure, a weakness or threat and lesser emphasis on perceived success, strength and opportunity.

Binocular trick makes us blow a negative assumption out of proportion, which becomes extremely distressing. This tendency is called, "Catastrophization." Here is an example: you have done a minor mistake in your workplace and now you fearing that you might lose your job as a consequence." When you catch yourself engaging in a binocular trick, say to yourself, "I recognize this thought pattern. This is a binocular trick. I'm going to take some deep breaths and allow myself to calm down. Overanalyzing is paralyzing. I choose to think rationally".

Emotional Reasoning

When we are overwhelmed with anxiety, negative emotions cloud our thinking. We start to believe that what we feel must be true. Emotional reasoning is a negative thinking pattern that substitutes emotion for evidence. Most of the negative thought patterns can be broken using rational statements, but emotional reasoning is quite challenging to break. The basic assumption for emotional reasoning is, " if there is smoke, there must be fire " . Here is an example, " I feel guilty, therefore I must have done something wrong"

If you catch yourself indulging in emotional reasoning, remind yourself to question the feeling and find out if the feeling tells the truth. Say to yourself, " I'm not going to let emotional reasoning cloud my judgments. Feelings often lie. I'm going to fact-check before accepting something as true."

Should and must statements

Sometimes being unapologetic will help you to beat your anxiety. When we are anxious, we make statements to ourselves using the phrases that contain should or must. Here are some examples: " I should not annoy my co-workers by asking for help". Or "my boss did not reply to my sick day email. He must be upset at me". These statements arise as the emotional consequence of guilt. When our anxiety makes us direct should or must statement towards others, or ourselves we feel irritated, guilty, resentful or frustrated. These statements often surface automatically, out of our awareness and we unwittingly use these statements as a way to take on a pessimistic view in our lives. This often causes a great deal of emotional distress. If you find yourself making should or must statements because of anxiety, say to yourself, " I recognize this thought pattern. This is "using should or must". I'm going to let go these thoughts and relax a bit. Everything is going to be fine."

Labeling and mislabeling

This is another thinking pattern that motivates us to focus on the negative aspects of life. Anxiety often ruins our self-esteem, and as a result, we tend to frequently label ourselves and others with demeaning labels. Labeling and mislabeling is overgeneralization at its worst. This negative mindset is developed from the self-image based on the errors we have made. Persistent anxiety can make us view ourselves as losers.

In most cases, people with this thinking pattern unconsciously nurture hostility, jealousy, and hatred, and label others negatively. Whenever you identify a labeling and mislabeling thought, say to yourself, "these demeaning labels are the products of anxiety. They don't describe others or me. These labels are not real, they are mislabels. I'm learning to forgive myself for all the mistakes I've made and move on with my life."

Personalization

Personalization makes people take things personally. In personalization, an anxiety sufferer may feel responsible for other's anger for failure, for bad weather, or for a host of uncontrollable circumstances. Teenagers with anxiety may suffer from guilt when their parents get divorced; because they believe it's their fault. People with severe personalization tendency may keep blaming themselves for virtually everything. When a crisis erupts, they immediately think, " I must have done something wrong ". They may obsessively keep reviewing the incident to find a reason to blame themselves. When you find yourself engaging in personalization, say to yourself, " I can recognize this thinking pattern. I'll never blame myself without convincing pieces of evidence".

Chapter 2

Relaxation: Why It Is So Important?

Anxiety triggers our sympathetic nervous system and creates a feeling of stiffness throughout our body and a storm of thoughts in our mind. When we practice relaxation, it activates the parasympathetic nervous system, which counteracts the distress we experience in our body and mind.

Have you ever paid attention to the physical symptoms while experiencing anxiety? Anxiety expresses itself through the physical symptoms. If you eliminate the physical aspects of anxiety, you can take its power away.

The physical symptoms of anxiety diminish when you relax your body. When the body becomes relaxed, your mind becomes calm. When our body and mind is settled, we feel in control. And all the negative forces of mind that try to take our peace away, disappear.

To manage anxiety, your goal should be relaxing the mind and body. You don't have to fight to attain relaxation— you only have to let go.

Every time you feel anxious, remember to relax. You may also whisper to yourself, "Relax" or "loosen up". In this chapter, we will discuss several relaxation technics. We'll start with breathing exercises.

Calm Breathing Exercise

The way we breathe changes the way we feel. Our breathing slows down when we feel calm. The breathing speeds up when we feel tense. But the opposite is also true. If you can deliberately slow down the process of breathing, it will pacify your mind. The following exercises are a quick fix for anxiety. Practicing all the exercises included in this chapter will give you temporary relief. But in order to achieve the lasting solution, you have to apply the cognitive and behavioral strategies included in this book.

You can practice breathing exercises anytime, anywhere. But practicing on an empty stomach can produce the best result. Whenever you feel anxious, practice these exercises sequentially; the result will be instantaneous. We will start with Diaphragmatic Breathing.

For this exercise (diaphragmatic breathing), sit down comfortably with your back straight or lie down comfortably with your knees bent and head supported. Use a flat and firm surface. You can place a pillow underneath your knees to feel more comfortable.

Now place your right hand below your belly button and left hand a couple of inches below your collar bone.

Now with your mouth closed a slow deep breath through your nose. Make sure your upper chest does not move as you breathe. Take the air inside your belly — and let your abdomen move out as you breathe in and fall as you breathe out.

Notice the difference between abdominal breathing and chest breathing. As you inhale, be aware as the air enters into your nose and the cool feeling.

As you exhale, instead of using your nose, exhale through your pursed lips and tighten your abdominal muscle as you empty your stomach.

Do it again: Breathe-in through the nose. Breathe-out through the mouth (pursed lips). Do it at least five more times.

The best time to practice abdominal breathing is in the morning before you start your day.

Our next exercise is a pranayama breathing technique. In yoga, breath is called "Prana" or the life force. Pioneers of yoga believed that by controlling our breath, we can bring our mind in control. The following exercise is called alternate nostril breathing or "Nodi Shodhan Pranayama".

Sit in an upright position. Now, block your right nostril with your thumb and inhale deeply with your left nostril, while mentally counting from one to five.

Now block your both nostrils with your index finger and thumb. Hold your breath until you count to five. Now exhale slowly — this time through your right nostril while mentally counting eight. Use your index finger to block your left nostril as you breathe out.

Hold your breath again and block both of your nostrils until you count to five.

This is one round. Do it again.

Here is the sequence···

Breathe-in (left): One···two········five.

Hold One···Two········Five.

Breathe Out (right): One···Two················Eight.

Hold One···Two········Five.

Do this exercise for at least two more times.

 Keep the flow natural and don't force -breathe. If this exercise is too advanced for you, you can skip holding your breath.

Relaxing Different Muscle Groups

Anxiety makes our muscles tensed. If you relax your muscles, you will relax your feelings. In this exercise, we'll learn how to calm the mind by progressively tensing and relaxing muscle groups throughout your entire body. This exercise will show you the difference between tensed and relaxed muscle so that you can recognize the physical feeling of anxiety the moment it arises.

To practice this exercise, sit or lie down in a comfortable posture. Make sure you won't be interrupted during the exercise session. This exercise will take 10 to 15 minutes; so make sure that you are not in a hurry. Wear comfortable clothing. Remove your shoes.

If practicing in a lying position makes you feel sleepy, practice in a sitting posture. Our goal is to learn to relax the body while awake.

Now take a long deep and slow breath through your abdomen. Hold it for five seconds, and exhale slowly. Breathe again and watch your body expands with inhalation. Breath out and notice that your body contracts with exhalation. Remember to maintain the natural breathing as you go through each step.

Now raise your eyebrows as high as you can. This will tighten the muscles in your forehead. Hold until you count from one to five, then release abruptly. As you release the tensed muscles in your forehead, notice that tension falls away as the muscles become loose. Pause for 10 seconds.

Smile as widely as you can, and tighten your cheek muscles. Hold to the count of five, then release. Feel the muscles of your cheek soften as you release the tension. Relax for ten seconds.

Now squint your eyelids tightly shut and tighten your eye muscles. Take care not to hurt yourself while tensing any part of your body. Make sure that you are applying gentle pressure. Hold for five seconds⋯ then release. Pause for 10 seconds. Then continue to work on all the other major muscle groups of your body:

- Mouth — Open your mouth wide enough to stretch the hinges of your jaw. After five seconds⋯release.

- Neck and shoulders— Bring your head back so that your chin pointing toward the ceiling. Hold to the count of five and relax. Contract your upper back by making your shoulder blades closer. Stay for five seconds, then release. Now lift your shoulders up closer to your ears. Hold for five seconds, and then let go. Feel the tension melts away as you loosen up the shoulder muscles, and remember to breathe naturally.

- Chest — Tighten your chest by taking a deep breath.
- Hands— Clench your both fists and hold to the count of five, then let go.
- Entire arms— Clench your fists and draw your both forearms towards your shoulders. Tighten your biceps and keep the pressure for five seconds. Then release.
- Stomach — Tighten your stomach muscles by sucking in. Stay for five seconds··· and let go. Make sure to maintain a 10-second pause between two relaxations.
- Buttocks— Tighten the muscles of your buttock by pulling together. Hold for five seconds. Then release. Remember to breathe normally as you contract and release each muscle group.

- Thighs and knees— Press your knees together and tighten your thighs. Keep the pressure for five seconds····. And let go.

- Feet— Flex your feet, pulling your toes toward the shins and feel the pressure in your calves. Maintain the tension for five seconds ···. then release. curl your toes toward the floor, tensing your feet. Hold for five seconds ··· and release.

Your whole body is relaxed now. Breathe in deeply and exhale slowly. Take a couple more breaths before you end this exercise.

The Laughing Cure

It's true that a good sense of humor can't heal all illnesses, but data is mounting about the physical and mental benefits of laughter. There are immense short-term benefits of good laughter. Reliving anxiety is one of them.

Laughter reduces the secretion of stress hormones adrenaline and cortisol and triggers release of endorphins and oxytocin. It stimulates the feeling of caring, forgiveness, and love, which overpowers the sad feeling of anxiety. Laughter elevates the free flow of emotions, hence dislodges blocked emotions, unresolved conflicts stored in the bottom of the unconscious mind. The release of blocked emotions and unresolved conflicts liberates the mind from unwanted emotions. Laughter is a wonderful non-violent method for emotional release and catharsis. It soothes the soul, works as a natural antidote for anxiety, stress, and depression

In yoga, there is a practice called Hasyayoga or laughter yoga, which involves prolonged voluntary laughter. This practice is based on the principle that forced laughter provides the same physical and mental benefits as spontaneous laughter. When this exercise is done in groups, maintaining eye contact, it soon becomes contagious and turns into real laughter.

This laughing exercise is about letting go all your inhibitions and laugh like a child.

It is a wonderful way to let go all the negative emotions and feel rejuvenated.

You can practice laughter yoga alone.

You can also find a partner or join a laughter yoga club or class in your area.

To do this exercise, start by clapping with your hands parallel to each other; it will increase your energy level by stimulating different acupressure points located in your hands.

Move around with clapping your hands with a 1-2-3 rhythm; you may move your hands up and down and swinging them from side to side as you clap. If you are practicing alone, you can do the warm-ups in front of the mirror.

There are different ways to perform warm-ups, you can clap hands, talk gibberish or swindle the tongue.

Start quietly, and then increase the volume, as you get comfortable. Lion laughter is also a good warm-up. To do it correctly, open your mouth and stick your tongue out fully; stretch your hands out like the paws of a lion. Make a roaring sound; then laugh from your belly.

Now in rhythm with your hands, say your first chant, "ho ho, ha-ha-ha" while breathing in and out deeply from your belly. You may continue clapping and chanting as you move around in a room in a circle.

Increase the volume of your laughter, as you get more comfortable.

Instructors can use different techniques to make this exercise more fruitful like greeting laughter technique, where the participants walk around the room and greet each other with laugh; or argument laughter where the participants are divided into two groups, then look at each other, point at each other and laugh louder at each other with belly laughs. The participants can laugh with holding hands or hugging each other. Gradually the laughter winds down, and the practitioners enter into a state of deep relaxation.

Maintain a sense of childlike playfulness as you practice laughter yoga. Laugh on a daily basis, ideally, in the morning, teach your body and mind to laugh on command. You may find it little difficult and feel discouraged in the beginning, keep up your practice, and soon you will start to enjoy it.

Mindful Jogging

Anxiety often makes us feel immobilized. If we get physically active, we can immediately get some relief. Researchers found that physical exercise can treat mild to moderate anxiety and depression as efficiently as antidepressant medications- but without harming the body.

To get the emotional benefits of physical exercise, you don't have to do strenuous workouts. Instead, do some jogging every day for thirty minutes— you will be amazed by the result.

When anxiety strikes, our system floods with adrenaline, cortisol and other stress hormones. When these hormones are released, our sympathetic nervous system becomes unstable; we feel distressed and experience physical discomforts. The best way to get rid of adrenaline is to burn it off with cardiovascular exercises, like running/jogging or aerobics.

Burning adrenaline and other stress hormones are not the only improve the anxiety condition. When we jog, our system releases neurochemicals like endorphins. Endorphins work like analgesics, which interact with the receptors of the brain and shrink the perception of emotional pain. Endorphins also contain sedative properties; they work like morphine and triggers a positive feeling in the body and mind. But unlike morphine, body's endorphins don't lead to addiction. Our body also releases other happy hormones like oxytocin, serotonin and reward hormone dopamine when we jog.

To get the most out of your jogging program, learn to do it mindfully. Mindful jogging is about enjoying the exercise with your senses. For mindful jogging, choose a place with the least visual distraction. Avoid crowded places or heavy traffic. Be aware of the environment, the temperature, and the sound. As you jog, feel the movements of your leg-joints and tension in the calf muscles; feel as your calf muscles and hamstrings stretch and contract with every movement. Feel the rhythm from heel to toe. Stay present; be aware as you breathe in and out.

We will discuss more about mindfulness later in this book.

If you do jogging every day, it will help change the way you feel and put you in a better mood.

Chapter 3

Transforming Intrusive Thoughts

When we feel overwhelmed with anxiety, our mind races with negative thoughts.

We try our best to fight or run away from those negative intrusive thoughts. But that only makes them stronger. There is a better strategy for dealing with those intrusive thoughts. Which is turning them into rational and realistic statements. Here some examples.

1. My feeling is making me restless and uncomfortable, but I can handle it.

2. I know fighting only makes my anxiety more powerful — I choose not to fight. Anxiety shrinks when I quit fighting.

3. Although I'm feeling a little uncomfortable, I can still focus on the task in hand. By staying

present and focused on my task, my anxiety decreases.

4. Although I'm feeling tense, I can still relax.

5. My anxiety wants me to rush, but I know, this is not an emergency. I can take all the time I need to let go and relax.

6. I can use this feeling as an opportunity for me to learn to cope with my fears. The more I learn, the more powerful I become.

7. The symptoms I'm experiencing right now is uncomfortable, but it is not dangerous. It can't hurt me.

8. I've survived every time I went through this feeling, and I will survive this time too.

9. I have developed this habit of being upset. I'll break this habit pattern eventually. I feel a little bit of peace despite my anxiety. This peace will grow and my anxiety will disappear.

I only have to stick to my practice and wait patiently.

10.   My attention makes anxiety stronger. If I don't pay attention to anxiety, it will shrink. Anxiety wants my attention because it will not survive without it.

The Mindful Way

Learning the mindful way will help you to make peace with anxious feelings. This will improve the quality of your life. Mindfulness will generate a sense of acceptance. When you truly become mindful of your thoughts, feelings, and sensations, you'll embrace them without judgment and criticism. This will diminish the power of your anxiety. To learn the mindful way, you have to practice mindfulness meditation.

So prepare yourself for the practice. You'll need a quiet place. If the environment is not perfectly quiet, that's fine. We can use noise and distraction as a part of our meditation. You can turn on some gentle music if you like.

Sit comfortably with your back straight (not stiff) and chin up. If you're sitting on the chair, keep your legs uncrossed with your feet touching the floor.

It is good to meditate in the same place at the same time every day.

It is important to touch joy and happiness while practicing mindfulness. So meditate with a little smile on your face.

When you are ready, close your eyes and take a few moments to gather your attention by simply being fully present with your breath as it enters and leaves your body.

Rest your attention on your nostrils where you feel the inflow and the outflow. Notice as you breath-in through your nostrils, you feel cool. As you breathe out, you feel warm. Become aware of the feeling of coolness and warmth as the air moves in and out.

Normal breathing is effortless. Pay your attention to this spontaneous movement of your breathing cycle. Escort your awareness to the place in your body where you clearly experience the process of breathing.

Now shift our attention on your belly. Notice your belly expands with inhalation and contracts with exhalation. Also, pay attention to the way each breath changes.

Sometimes thoughts will drift your mind away from your breath. Every time you feel lost in thoughts, remind yourself to re-connect with the natural rhythm— and gently drift back.

Maintain the effortless breathing and remain present throughout the whole sequence of inhaling, exhaling and pausing between breaths.

The process of paying attention should be effortless. It should not affect the natural rhythm of your breathing. Pay effortless attention and relax into each breath. Sustain your attention throughout the entire breath-cycle— one breath at a time.

Notice the sensation when each breath arises until the next breath begins. In this meditation practice, your breath is the anchor for your attention. Therefore every time your mind moves away, escort it back to your breath.

The rhythm of your breathing will change automatically. Sometimes your breath will be long, sometimes short, and sometimes shallow. Be aware of the change and allow it to be the way it is.

After a couple of minutes, shift your awareness from breath to sounds as they spontaneously call your attention to them and away from your breath.

Become aware of the sounds inside or outside the room. It could be the sound of clock or birds twittering or distant traffic— whatever it is focus on the sound without bothering about the source.

Pay attention to space between sounds. The space is silence. Be aware of the silence.

Expand your awareness to become present with the subtle sounds as they arise from all directions. Let them arise spontaneously in your consciousness. You don't have to think about the source or cause of the sound, let the sounds be known spontaneously.

If you find yourself thinking about the sounds, gently shift your attention to their sensory characteristics such as loudness, pitch, and frequency.

Notice your reaction as a sound enters into your consciousness. Notice if the mind terms the sound as pleasant or unpleasant. You don't need to change or resist anything. You only have to observe.

Whenever a thought shifts your attention from the sound to something else, calmly move your attention back to the sounds as they rise and fall from one moment to the next.

After a few minutes, when the sound no longer holds your attention, direct your focus on your bodily sensations. Every time boredom creeps in, return to the anchor— your breath.

Notice the sensations you're experiencing right now in your entire body. Move your focus to the quality of the sensation.

Is it a feeling of tension or numbness? Whatever it is, be present with that sensation.

Observe if any change occurs the moment you focus your attention on a sensation of your body. Is there any clinging or avoiding tendency? See how accurately you can recognize each sensation as it enters into your awareness.

Don't judge your sensations. Just observe as the rise, peak, and fall.

Notice if your attention amplifies the sensation or weaken it or make it shrink.

There is no need to change the way you feel. Our goal is not to change anything. Becoming fully aware is the goal. Sensations are transient. They will fade.

The sensations of anxiety are also temporary— it will also disappear in time.

Now include the awareness of emotion in your practice. Emotions will inevitably arise in your consciousness.

The moment an emotion surfaces into your awareness, recognize the emotion and accept it nonjudgmentally.

Stay in a receptive mood as you become aware of your emotional state. Remain open and permit yourself to be completely present with the emotion. Direct all your attention to fully experience the emotion.

Human mind terms an emotion as pleasant or unpleasant or neutral. It clings to pleasant emotions and pushes away the negative ones. Whenever the emotion appears in your awareness, simply let it remain in your awareness without pursuing it.

Some emotions can be a bit tricky to navigate.

If a strong emotion appears in your mind, open to a mindful inquiry, reflecting on the nature of the emotion itself, without becoming involved in the story.

Label your emotions. For instance, if you feel irritated, you can label it "anger", if feel sad, label as " grief " or " Sadness " . Allow yourself to fully experience the emotion. Contain the emotion.

 Being mindful of the emotion is the most important part of your mindfulness practice; because it will change your relationship with negative emotions.

If you can become mindful of anxious feelings, you no longer have to resist it. You'll only accept it with a non-reactive awareness.

In the final stage, we're going to practice Choiceless awareness. Become aware of everything that arises in the background of our consciousness. Whether it is sound, thoughts, images, sensation or emotion, you'll allow it to remain there, focusing primarily on the flow of your breathing. If a sound predominates the background of your awareness, make it a focus of your attention. If a thought, image or sensation predominates the background, make it your object to focus and expand your field of awareness to include the entire range of experience — breath, sounds, thoughts, images, sensations, and emotions.

Now it is time to end your practice. Don't come out too quickly. Take your time. Become aware that you're going to end your meditation. Slowly open your eyes.

Gently move your upper body. Stretch your hands and legs. Then stand up.

Chapter 4

The Action Phase

In the last three chapters, we mostly worked on cognitive aspects of anxiety. In order to make the lasting change, we also have to work on the behavioral aspect. We will discuss two exposure techniques in this chapter — flooding and implosion. These are behavioral fear exposure strategies, which involve facing your own fears. I know, if you have persistent anxiety, even the thought of staring your worst fears in the face can make you terrified. But rest assured, it is not as fearful as it sounds. Although this technique will put you in direct contact with your object of fear, it is perfectly safe. I'm not going to ask you to endanger yourself to overcome the fear of height or wild animals.

These techniques involve a systematic, gradual set of steps that you can handle one at a time.

Once you learn a step, you will move to the next step.

A new step will bring some degree of anxiety, but not more than you can manage.

It is important not to procrastinate with the instructions of flooding and implosion.

If you find yourself procrastinating with action steps, go back to previous chapters to prepare yourself mentally.

If you still find these techniques extremely anxiety producing, seek professional help. It is advised not to try these methods when your anxiety is high. Facing fears with high anxiety often does harm than good. Also, don't try these methods if you are dealing with other disorders such as alcoholism and substance abuse. Therapists often recommend exposure in combination with medication for severely anxious individuals.

Before trying each action step relax your body and mind by doing breathing exercises. You can try abdominal breathing or alternate nostril breathing or both. You can even do mindful meditation for 10 minutes. If muscular relaxation technique puts you into a more relaxed state, you can try it too.

Before attempting facing your fears, break up the process into small manageable steps. The way you break up your fears will give you an idea of the nature of your fear perception. Here is how to do it. Start with listing the objects of your anxiety.

For instance, you might be afraid of one of the following:

- Meeting new people
- Heights
- Traveling to new places

- Financial loss

Pick one object from your list and think about every conceivable aspect of your fear.

Now, in your mind's eye, envision a situation that includes an object of your fear. Imagine all the activities that surround that object and find out when the fear starts.

As, for example, you are afraid of social events and you are starting to feel anxious as you are traveling to that location. Or perhaps the fear starts the moment you step into a room filled with people. Take note of whenever the fear begins.

Next step is anticipating all possible outcomes. Include all the small details, such as people's reaction, or what they might think about you.

Now ask yourself the following questions:

- Exactly when did I start feeling anxious?

- Which part of the event could produce the highest level of anxiety?

- Which are the activities I tend to avoid?

- If I have to face my fear head on, what are the things I will do?

- If I have to go through the most fearful part of the event, do I have any crutches? If so, what are they?

- What is the worst outcome I could anticipate if I were to confront my fear?

Take time to think and write your honest answers. You don't have to feel embarrassed to explain the darkest aspects of your fear, which you think may sound stupid to others.

Exploring your worst fear can make feel a little anxious. Take a deep breath in and out for a few times, then move on. The next step is designing your fear ladder.

Designing Your Fear ladder

Now you have some understanding of the nature of your fear. In this stage, you'll take your fear apart by building a fear ladder. Here are the steps to follow:

- Write down all the activities you'll sequentially follow to ultimately face your fear.

- Rate each activity on a scale of 0 to 100.

- Arrange the items in a ladder beginning with the lowest rated item at the bottom and highest rated item on the top stair. This ladder is your 'exposure hierarchy', another term used for the fear ladder. Creating the fear ladder may cause anxiety in some people. If it happens, take a few deep breaths and continue. Don't worry; you won't face all the items at once. We will take one step at a time.

See the following example. It's a fear ladder for facing the fear of social situations.

Giving a speech or being a center of attention	93
Getting introduced to someone	88
Talking to an attractive men/women	84
Commuting to the event	78
Doing handshakes with people I don't know	70
Unexpectedly seeing someone I know	50
Talking to people I know	45
Preparing myself for the event	35

The above ladder contains 8 steps. You can break the task into 16 or more steps if you like. For example, you can add an in-between step or two such as parking at the garage or being greeted by the host.

Make your own fear ladder. Before finally facing your fear we are going to do a visualization exercise.

Imagining Your Fear

The best preparation for exposing yourself in your anxiety-triggering situation is visualization practice. Because when you visualize your fear, you will experience less anxiety than facing it for real. You may think that imagining your fear won't make you anxious at all. But most people who were asked to vividly imagine a stressful event reported anxiety symptoms when they visualized rich details of the event. The most important benefit of visualization is that through imagining people gradually master their fear in the mind and feel less anxious before they face the object of fear in reality.

Here are the basic steps of visualization exercise:

1. First, do some breathing exercises.

2. Start with the lowest step of your fear ladder

3. Visualize as if you are really facing your fear.

4. Feel if it is real. Bring color, smell, sound, texture, and touch. Vividly imagine all the sensory features. Don't visualize like you are watching a video. Imagine as the first person. Don't try hard to be perfect. It may take some practice to construct a clear picture.

5. When you have the picture in your mind of the event of fear, rate the level of anxiety on a scale of 0 to 100.

6. Maintain your attention on the picture until your anxiety fades. For instance, if you experience anxiety level 90, stay with the picture until it drops to 40.

7. Before ending your visualization session breath-in and out deeply for a few times.

8. If your imagination was vivid and you constructed a clear picture and everything

went easily, you can move to the next phase of exposure.

Facing Fear Head On

After practicing visualization you'll notice your anxiety level has reduced. Now you're better prepared to take the plunge. You have already broken down your fears into small steps. Now you'll face them face them head-on starting from the least problematic to the most intensely feared. Follow the steps below:

1. Breath in and out deeply three times.

2. Pick the idea from the bottom of your ladder. If you think you can accept a bigger challenge, choose the one that causes a moderate level of anxiety.

3. You are free to break the fear further into a small number of sequential steps. But you're not allowed to procrastinate.

4. There is no need to hurry or be hard on yourself. Take one step at a time and continue working on each step until anxiety fades significantly (less than 40 percent).

The moment you notice a rise of your anxiety level, breath in and out slowly for a few times. The following tips can help you.

- If you get help from a friend during this procedure, that's fine.

- You have a choice to take a step back if your fear is high. But don't retreat completely unless you feel completely out of control. Don't give up easily

- Become aware of the voice of anxiety. This voice knows many ticks. It will try to discourage you. It may tell you that nothing will work. Just ignore it.

- Reward yourself upon the successful completion of each step. Buy yourself a treat.

- Use the thought replacement technique to manage the negative self-talk.

- You may feel uncomfortable at times. It is part of the process.

- Always remember to breathe deeply when the anxiety level gets high. Use the words, "relax" or "loosen up" to ease your mind and body.

- Be present with the object of fear until your anxiety drops.

- Make sure your goals are realistic. For instance, if public speaking is your worst fear, setting a goal of presenting to a large group of 300 is not realistic.

- Face your fears with a clear mind and avoid crutches. Common crutches may include, drinking alcohol, taking antidepressant medications (e.g. benzodiazepines) and using distractions like songs, rituals etc. Crutches may reduce your anxiety level, but it may affect the effectiveness of this procedure.

Closing Comments

Your anxiety took years to develop. Overcoming it will take a while. So be patient and stick to your practice. Never beat yourself up for slow progress. Sometimes anxiety returns after a few successful exposures to the same stressful event. Remember, setbacks are the part of the process. Having setbacks is a sign of progress. Take your time to accomplish all the steps. But make sure you are making progress. Methods discussed in this book are quite effective if you practice sincerely. Practice and persistence will eventually enable you to triumph over your anxiety.

Enjoy Your Life !

Made in the
USA
Monee, IL